THE UNOFFICIAL

Liberal
Joke★Book

BOB PHILLIPS

Illustrated by Nate Owens

HARVEST HOUSE PUBLISHERS
Eugene, Oregon 97402

"This Is the Introduction" is adapted from *Humor Is Tremendous* by Charlie T. Jones and Bob Phillips (Wheaton, IL: Tyndale House Publishers, 1988). Used by permission.

THE UNOFFICIAL LIBERAL JOKE BOOK

Illustrations by Nate Owens
Edited by Hugh Caldwell

Library of Congress Cataloging-in-Publication Data

Phillips, Bob, 1940–
    The unofficial liberal joke book : for the politically incorrect / Bob Phillips.
      p. cm.
    ISBN 1-56507-278-2
    1. Liberalism—United States—Humor.   I. Title.
  PN6231.L47P48   1994
  818'.540208—dc20
                                         94-14574
                                             CIP
                                             Rev.

Printed in the United States of America.

94   95   96   97   98   99   00   01 — 10   9   8   7   6   5   4   3   2   1

Before You Rush In...

Two Democrats and their very liberal friend were walking along the beach, when one of them spotted a magic lamp that had washed ashore. The first Democrat grabbed it, gave it a rub, and out popped a genie. Says the genie, "I will grant you each one wish." The first Democrat said, "I want to be 50 times smarter and more clever." "No problem," said the genie. "Poof! You're 50 times smarter and more clever." Away walked the Democrat, quite contented.

The second Democrat turned to the genie and said, "I want to be 500 times smarter and more clever than the last guy." "No problem," said the genie. "Poof! You're 500 times smarter and more clever than that first guy." And away he went, ecstatic with joy.

The very liberal friend wanted to make sure he got the best wish of all. He thought for a moment and said, "I want to be *10,000* times smarter and more clever than any Democrat who has ever lived!"

"That's a pretty tall order," said the genie. "Are you sure?"

"Yep," said the liberal.

Questioned the genie, "I'm not sure you understand the consequences. Are you *positive?"*

"Yes, I'm POSITIVE!" insisted the man.

"OK," said the genie. "Poof! You're Rush Limbaugh."

Rush recently went to dinner with Ted Kennedy. When the waiter arrived, Rush said, "I'd like the biggest, reddest T-bone steak you have."

"And for the vegetable?" said the waiter.

"He'll have the same thing," said Rush.

Rush has a great reputation as a fisherman. Rarely does he not limit out. Phil Donahue wanted to know his secret and asked Rush if he could go along on his next fishing trip. Rush agreed, and the next day they loaded into a boat and rowed out to the middle of a lake. Setting aside his fishing pole, Rush reached into a sack and pulled out a huge stick of dynamite. He lit the fuse and tossed it into the lake. *KA-BOOM!* Several fish floated to the surface.

Donahue was irate. "You can't do that! Don't you care about the *environment?*" Rush pulled out another stick and lit it. Tossing it in Donahue's lap, he said, "Look, are we going to talk, or are we going to fish?"

After enjoying his fish dinner, Rush decided to take a stroll in the woods. Spotting a young leprechaun, Rush grabbed him as he walked by.

"Oh please, Mr. Limbaugh, if you let me free, I will grant you any wish," said the leprechaun.

Rush pulled out a map of the United States. "I'd wish to own a beautiful estate in all 50 states."

"If only I could," said the leprechaun sadly, "but I'm still a leprechaun trainee. I haven't learned how to do that yet. Is there something else I can grant you?"

Rush paused and thought. "I guess I'd settle for the name of one Democratic politician who could be trusted to keep his promises."

"Hmmm," responded the leprechaun. "Lemme see that map again."

Tom Corwin wrote that "to keep the machinery of government operating efficiently, it must be oiled frequently with fun and laughter; otherwise friction and hate will soon wear it out." I hope that Rush and his many followers will enjoy this tongue-in-cheek poke of fun at Rush's two favorite targets: the Democrats and the liberals.

Peter DeVries said that the satirist shoots to kill while the humorist brings his prey back to life, eventually releasing him to "capture" another chance at him. Rush is that humorist who loves to capture the Democrats and liberals time and time again. It is to Rush and his manner of humor that I dedicate this joke book.

—Bob Phillips
Fresno, California

P.S. Personally, I'm against liberal political jokes. But that doesn't seem to prevent them from getting elected.

This Is the Introduction

HUMOR IS TREMENDOUS. It adds sparkle and zest to one's life. It helps us learn to laugh at the world, ourselves, and others. It helps us not take life too seriously.

Humor can be very useful. It can be a form of entertainment or a method for reducing tension. Ideas and concepts become more memorable when humor is used. Humor helps to clarify important points. Humor can persuade and convince others to take action. Humor can lift people for a breath of air when the subject is serious. Humor encourages us to accept truth more easily.

Many people have problems with humor. They don't perceive themselves as funny, or they've never had any luck telling jokes. Here are some frequently heard comments or questions about humor, along with my response.

I just can't remember jokes. I always forget the punch line.

There are two ways to remember jokes. The first is to write down the joke shortly after you hear it. The second is to share the joke with someone shortly after you hear it. Telling the joke will reinforce it in your memory. The old maxim is true: "We only keep what we give away."

I just can't tell jokes.

Telling jokes is like every other activity in life: If you want to be good at it, you have to practice. Start by telling simple one-line jokes or puns. As you gain success, move on to longer jokes and stories.

Does a good joke always get a laugh?

No, it does not. Response varies with the audience, the delivery of the joke, the time of day, and many other factors. Physical factors are important. For example, if the lighting in the room is dim, the audience won't see the twinkle in your eye. And not every joke is appropriate for every audience. Telling a funeral joke to a group in which someone has recently passed away will cause the death of your joke.

What makes a joke funny?

Many times, humor is in the eye of the beholder. Humor can be likened to a magic trick that is performed with words. It involves an obvious untruth or exaggeration, and it contains a surprise or a punch line or an unexpected twist. It is made up of the *setup* and the *payoff.* The payoff is the revelation or punch line that pulls it all together.

It seems like many jokes have targets. They seem to pick on people or attack them.

This is true. Humor often pokes fun at bosses, government, authority figures, and various groups. People don't mind if you hit a target— just don't wipe it out.

What happens when the joke or story fails?

The first thing is to learn to die with dignity by acknowledging the "bomb." The second thing to do is to profit by it. Examine why the joke did not work. Ask yourself:

★ Was the delivery poor?

★ Was it targeted for the wrong audience?

★ Was it a failure to stress the punch line properly and clearly?

★ Was it a failure of timing?

★ Was the pace too fast or too slow?

Telling jokes can be a lot of fun. Or it can be a disaster, like the man who told a joke and everyone booed except one man: He was applauding the booing.

If you would like to guarantee disaster in your joke telling, follow these suggestions:

1. Make sure you forget the punch line; sadists enjoy a letdown.

2. Laugh at your own joke and be sure to jab your audience during the process. Be sure to slap them on the back, too.

3. Tell the same story over if the point is missed. This will assure at least wry smiles.

4. Make sure the story is long enough to lull the dull ones to sleep.

5. Tell the wrong joke to the wrong audience; they'll feel worse than you do.

6. Above all else, don't be yourself, because you know you're not humorous even if you are funny.

If, on the other hand, you would like to have some measure of success in joke telling—ignore the above six suggestions.

One of the great delusions in the world is
the hope that the evils in this world
are to be cured by legislation.

THOMAS B. REED

Following a heated campaign debate,
two men from opposite political camps
hurriedly left the meeting hall, hoping
to beat the traffic. Driving in opposite
directions, their cars met and tires
screeched as they came to a halt inches
apart in the narrow parking lot. The liberal
leaned out and shouted, "I never back
up for a TOTAL MORON!"

"No worry," said the conservative,
shifting into reverse, "I ALWAYS DO!"

★★★

I always believed that fish was
"brain food" until I heard that
Ted Kennedy eats fish every day.

★★★

★

The Republicans have their splits right after
the election . . . and the Democrats have
theirs just before an election.

WILL ROGERS

★★★

I never said all Democrats were saloon-
keepers. What I said was that all
saloon-keepers were Democrats.

HORACE GREELEY

★★★

It has been said there are two things that
are unavoidable . . . death and taxes.
But I'm not sure that death gets worse
each time Congress meets.

★★★

Never underestimate the ability
of the Democrats to wet their finger
and hold it to the wind.

RONALD REAGAN

★★★

A Democrat was announcing his candidacy for Congress. "I have heard the voice of the people calling me to my destiny in public service!"

An unpersuaded heckler stood and shouted, "As empty as this hall is, how do you know it wasn't your echo?"

★★★

Liberals! They're not leaders! If they were real leaders they'd understand that their style of politicking and self-aggrandizement is what's destroying the capacity of any of us to get anywhere.

**DEMOCRATIC CONGRESSWOMAN
BELLA ABZUG**

★★★

There's no trick to being a humorist when you have the whole government working for you.

WILL ROGERS

★★★

When a liberal Congressman was campaigning, he hired a dozen research assistants—one to dig up the facts, the other 11 to bury them as deeply as possible.

★★★

I finally figured out why I'm constantly so exhausted. A recent survey found I was doing more than my share of the world's work. The population of the country is 260 million, but there are 78 million over 65 years of age. That leaves 182 million to do the work. People that are still in school are another 94 million which leaves 88 million to do the work. Then there are 33 million employed by the federal government leaving 55 million to do the work. 20 million more are in the Armed Services, leaving 35 million to do the work. Now deduct 25 million, the number of state, county, and city employees, and that leaves 10 million to do the work. Deduct 7 million people looking for work, and another 2.7 million on public assistance who *refuse* to work and that leaves just 300,000. There are 228,000 employed in medical and mental hospitals. Now we're down to 72,000.

It may interest you to know there are 71,998 people in federal, state, and local jails, leaving only *TWO PEOPLE* to do all the work. That would be me and that lazy good-for-nothing Democrat over there . . . and I'm getting pretty dog-tired doing all his work, too.

★★★

Practical politics consists
in ignoring facts.
HENRY ADAMS

★★★

Money may not go as far as
it used to, but it definitely
gets there *much* faster.

★★★

Two men took a shortcut through a graveyard and noticed a gravestone that read, "HERE LIES A LIBERAL AND A GOOD MAN."

"Imagine that!" said the one to the other. "I had no idea you could bury two men in one grave!"

"Imagine that—two men buried
in one grave!"

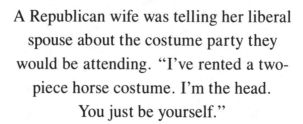

A Republican wife was telling her liberal spouse about the costume party they would be attending. "I've rented a two-piece horse costume. I'm the head. You just be yourself."

★★★

The perfect bureaucrat everywhere is the man who manages to make no decisions and escape all responsibility.

BROOKS ATKINSON

★★★

As a women's libber made her way to the back of a bus, a man stood up. "Listen, you chauvinist pig," she shrieked, "how dare you perpetuate the stupid myth that women are delicate creatures that you must indulge! I *demand* that you sit down immediately!"

"Make all the demands you want, lady," said the man, "I get off at this stop."

★★★

Full of self-congratulation, a newly elected Democrat Congressman was sitting at his new fancy desk in his new office. A young man approached his door, and the Congressman felt the urge to make a big impression, so he quickly picked up his phone and announced loudly, "No problem, Mr. President. Yes, you're welcome. I look forward to dinner with you and the First Lady tonight. Goodbye, sir."

Smugly turning to the young man he barked, "And what do *you* want? Can't you see I'm *very* busy?"

"I'm sorry, sir," apologized the young man. "I just came to install your phone."

"Reelection time will soon be here again," said the incumbent liberal Democrat. "Soon, the air will be filled with my famous speeches."

Responded his Republican colleague, "And vice versa."

★★★

Two men met at a party. "I'm a criminal lawyer," said the first.

"Isn't that *redundant?*" replied the other.

Outside of traffic, there is nothing that has held this country back as much as committees.

WILL ROGERS

Both thespians and liberal politicians make their living in make-believe worlds. The difference is, actors know it.

Liberalism seems to be related to the distance people are from the problem.

WHITNEY M. YOUNG, JR.

★★★

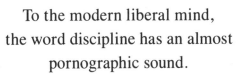

To the modern liberal mind,
the word discipline has an almost
pornographic sound.

DONALD BARR

Under the Clinton health plan, a liberal
having his conscience removed is classified
as a minor operation.

★★★

When I was young, they taught us *anyone*
could become president. I've recently
come to realize how utterly true that is.

★★★

We do not elect our wisest and best men to
represent us. In general, we elect men
of the type that subscribes to only
one principle—to get re-elected.

TERRY M. TOWNSEND

★★★

President Clinton was debating his new budget plan with Rush Limbaugh. "What if I told you that my plan calls for lower taxes, lower interest *and* unemployment rates, stimulation of the economy, provision of national health insurance, and *still* will be able to balance the budget?"

"I wouldn't say *one word*," answered Rush.

"You!" said Clinton tauntingly, "the great *RUSH LIMBAUGH* wouldn't have *anything* to say? That would be a first!"

"Well," explained Rush, "don't you know it's next to *impossible* to talk when you're doubled over in a laughing fit?"

A Democrat Congressman was being introduced to a local Rotary Club. "Tonight's speaker will not bore you with a long speech," said the host.

Returned a shout from the back, "He usually does it with a short one!"

★★★

In my youth, I, too, entertained some
illusions; but I soon recovered from them.
The great orators who rule the
assemblies by the brilliancy of their
eloquence are in general men of the most
mediocre political talents: they
should not be opposed in their own way; for
they have always more noisy words at
command than you. Their eloquence should
be opposed by a serious and logical
argument; their strength lies in vagueness;
they should be brought back to the
reality of facts; practical arguments destroy
them. In the council, there were men
possessed of much more eloquence than I
was; I always defeated them by this
simple argument—two and two makes four.

NAPOLEON

★★★

Our liberal Congressmen spend half their
time being witty. The half-wits.

★★★

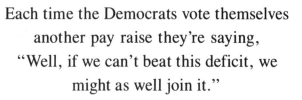

Each time the Democrats vote themselves
another pay raise they're saying,
"Well, if we can't beat this deficit, we
might as well join it."

★★★

An appropriation was a tangible thing, if
you got hold of it, and it made little
difference what it was appropriated for,
so long as you got hold of it.

MARK TWAIN

★★★

What this country needs is more
unemployed politicians.

EDWARD LANGLEY

★★★

Could there be a thinner book than
*The Liberal's Handbook of
Moral & Ethical Standards & Practices?*

★★★

A liberal said to his conservative co-worker, "I suppose you think I'm a perfect idiot."

"Oh," replied his friend, "I would never use the word 'perfect.' But at your current pace, it won't be long now."

★★★

I don't think it does any harm just once in a
while to acknowledge that the whole
country isn't in flames, that
there are people in the country besides
politicians, entertainers, and criminals.

CHARLES KURALT

★★★

You'll find that all of us individually have
the courage to make a tough decision.
The problem is to find 25 senators
who have that courage simultaneously.

SENATOR ROBERT (BOB) KERREY

★★★

The Navy honored President Clinton
by naming their new battleship the
USS Chicken of the Sea.

A liberal Democrat Congresswoman was lunching with a conservative colleague. "Where do you get off," she confronted him, "reading into the *Congressional Record* that I am deaf and dumb?"

Calmly responded her friend, "I *never* said you were deaf."

★★★

The campaign ends Tuesday,
but it will take two generations
to sweep up the dirt.

WILL ROGERS

★★★

A Republican was giving a speech in a rural district when a yokel tossed a cabbage at him. Ducking away, the quick-thinking Republican looked down at it on the platform. "It appears that while pondering the issues, my opponent has once again lost his head."

★★★

Ever hear about Ted Kennedy's speech school? He fills the students' mouths with marbles, which teaches them to better enunciate their words. Each day you lose one marble. When you've finally lost all your marbles, the Democrats run you for Congress.

★★★

When you say that you agree to a thing in principle, you mean that you have not the slightest intention of carrying it out in practice.

OTTO VON BISMARCK

★★★

A Democrat Senator complained to the Senate barber that his limo door had shut so fast that it bumped his crazy bone and raised quite a lump. Replied the barber, "Not to worry. I'll comb your hair over it so nobody will notice."

★★★

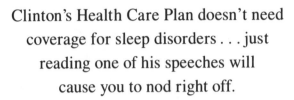

Clinton's Health Care Plan doesn't need
coverage for sleep disorders . . . just
reading one of his speeches will
cause you to nod right off.

★★★

I could study all my life and not think up
half the amount of funny things they
can think of in one session of Congress.

WILL ROGERS

★★★

When a liberal Congressman finally
finished an endless and tedious speech, you
could have heard a pin drop, except the
sound of one lone person clapping slowly.
Later he told his wife, "At least one
person appreciated what I had to say."

"I'm sorry," she apologized, "that was
me. I had to slap myself a few times to
wake myself up."

★★★

I have been a member of the House of
Representatives . . . twenty years. During
the whole of that time, we have been
attacked, denounced, despised, hunted,
harried, blamed, looked down upon,
excoriated, and flayed. I refuse to take it
personally. I have looked into
history. I find that we did not start being
unpopular when I became a
Congressman. We were unpopular when
Lincoln was a Congressman. We
were unpopular even when Henry Clay
was a Congressman. We have always been
unpopular. From the beginning of the
Republic it has been the duty of every free-
born voter to look down upon us, and
the duty of every free-born humorist
to make jokes at us.

NICHOLAS LONGWORTH

★★★

Politics ruins the character.

OTTO VON BISMARCK

★★★

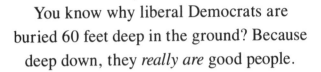

You know why liberal Democrats are buried 60 feet deep in the ground? Because deep down, they *really are* good people.

★★★

The principle of spending money to be paid by posterity under the name of funding, is but swindling futurity on a large scale.

THOMAS JEFFERSON

★★★

Of course my liberal Congressman offers sound advice. But with him that means offering 99 percent *sound* and 1 percent *advice*.

★★★

It's a terribly hard job to spend a billion dollars and get your money's worth.

GEORGE HUMPHREY

★★★

A Democrat Congressman asked his physician, "Doctor, do you think a person can live without a brain?"

"Well, I've read your comments on health care, so I consider you the living proof."

★★★

It isn't whether you win or lose but
how you place the blame.
CHUCK HOWE

★★★

The necessity of saying something, the
embarrassment produced by the
consciousness of having nothing to say,
and the desire to exhibit ability, are three
things sufficient to render
even a great man ridiculous.
VOLTAIRE

★★★

Dear Secretary of the Agriculture,

Mason Douglas, a farmer friend of mine, received a $25,000 check from the government for not raising hogs, which you believe will help the country. I want to get into the not raising hogs business, too.

Do you know what is the best kind of land to not raise hogs on, and what are the best kinds of hogs not to raise? I would prefer to not raise Razor Backs, but if this is not the best kind not to raise, I would be willing to not raise Durocs or Poland Chinas, too. How do you go about keeping records on each individual hog that is not raised?

Douglas has raised hogs for more than 20 years and never made more than $15,000, until this year when he got $25,000 for the 25 hogs he didn't raise. Now, if he gets $25,000 for not raising 25 hogs, can I get $50,000 for not raising 50 hogs? Or $200,000 for not raising 200 hogs? I plan to start off on a small scale, with only a few hundred hogs not raised, and then slowly build my farm till I'm not raising

800 or 1,000 hogs. (To make $1,000,000? Wow! What a great program!)

Now these hogs I won't raise won't eat *at least* 100,000 bushels of corn. I understand you also pay farmers for not growing corn. Will you pay me for not growing 100,000 bushels of corn, which I will not feed to the hogs which I am not raising? This would make for a very efficient operation: The hogs I won't raise won't be eating the corn I won't grow which won't be fertilized with the hog manure that isn't produced from the corn they won't be eating. What could be simpler, and more beneficial to the country (as you see it)?

Please contact me as soon as possible; I want to get started right away, as this looks like a great year for not raising hogs.

Yours very truly,
Lucas Lee

A recently retired and well-known
liberal sent his picture, autobiography,
and application to a Lonely Hearts Club.
A postcard came back: "We'll let you know
if we get that lonely."

"Thank you for showing interest in our club.
However, at this time we don't..."

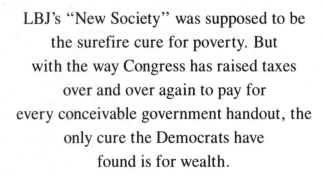

LBJ's "New Society" was supposed to be
the surefire cure for poverty. But
with the way Congress has raised taxes
over and over again to pay for
every conceivable government handout, the
only cure the Democrats have
found is for wealth.

★★★

A liberal lawyer couldn't decide if he
should see a palmist or a mind reader to
foretell his political future. He
asked his conservative father, and his
father said, "I have to say the palmist. I
know you have a palm."

★★★

"I must have a cold or something in my
head," sniffled the liberal to a coworker.
Laughed her friend, "Smart money's on
the cold."

★★★

Last night I slept like a Democrat
Congressman. First I lied on one side,
then I lied on the other.

★★★

I believe if we introduced
The Lord's Prayer here, Senators
would propose a large number of
amendments to it.

SENATOR HENRY WILSON

★★★

Since a politician never believes what
he says, he is surprised when
others believe him.

CHARLES DE GAULLE

★★★

Did you hear about Clinton's streamlined
tax form? Only *two* lines.
Line 1. What was your income last year?
Line 2. Send it in.

★★★

The dirty work at political conventions is almost always done in the grim hours between midnight and dawn. Hangmen and politicians work best when the human spirit is at its lowest ebb.

RUSSELL BAKER

★★★

Scientists from far and wide came to study the liberal Congressman who had received a baboon's brain when no human brains were available. They were amazed to find the only side effects were that he loved bananas, he had become far more sensible and even-tempered, and he could now get his legislation passed.

★★★

I am not a member of any organized party—I am a Democrat.

WILL ROGERS

★★★

An international visitor to Washington D.C. had become lost. "Excuse me, sir," he asked a man on the street, "can you tell me where the U.S. Capitol is?"

"All over the world, thanks to our Congress."

★★★

A young liberal boy just couldn't believe that a beautiful girl kept rejecting his advances. "Why won't you just go out on a simple little date? Is there someone else?"

Replied the girl, "Oh, dear Lord, there must be."

★★★

If I wanted to go crazy, I would do it in Washington because it would not be noticed.

IRWIN S. COBB

★★★

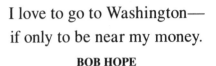

I love to go to Washington—
if only to be near my money.

BOB HOPE

★★★

During a college political debate, a
young Democrat spotted a very attractive
Republican coed. He tried to strike
up a conversation, but the girl was totally
unimpressed. The boy pleaded with
her, "Just what do I have to do to get one
little kiss from you?"

Thinking for a moment, she answered,
"You'd probably need to start with
chloroform. If that didn't work, you'd have
to try something stronger."

★★★

People ask me where I get my jokes.
Why, I just watch Congress and
report the facts; I don't even
have to exaggerate.

WILL ROGERS

★★★

The country has come to feel the same
when Congress is in session as when the
baby gets hold of a hammer.

WILL ROGERS

After giving a speech on the woes
of the environment, a young liberal
approached his speech professor. "Do you
think I could improve my speaking if I
practiced my enunciation with pebbles in
my mouth, just like Demosthenes?"

Retorted the professor, "In your case, I
recommend a quick-dry cement."

An IRS agent was attempting to reason
with a taxpayer. "Yes, I appreciate
your logic, and I certainly agree with you.
But I'm still afraid you cannot deduct
last year's taxes as a bad investment."

★★★

The new socialized Health Care Reform has been delayed due to the administration's effort to simplify the medical terminology into standard English. The following is a partial list of the translations:

Artery:	Study of paintings
Bacteria:	Rear door to the cafeteria
Barium:	What to do when the patient dies
Bowel:	A, E, I, O, U, (and sometimes) Y
Caesarean Section:	Roman neighborhood
Cat Scan:	Looking for kitty
Cauterize:	Made eye contact with her
Colic:	Kind of a dog
Coma:	Punctuation mark
Dilate:	Lived a real long time
Enema:	Not your friend
Fester:	Quicker
Fibula:	A small lie
Genital:	Not Jewish
G.I. Series:	Army baseball game
Hangnail:	Coat hook

Impotent:	Really valuable
Labor Pain:	Getting hurt at work
Medical staff:	The doctor's cane
Morbid:	A bigger offer
Nitrates:	Opposite of day rates
Node:	Became aware of
Outpatient:	Guy who fainted
Pelvis:	Elvis' cousin
Post-operative:	Mailman
Recovery room:	Where they do upholstery
Rectum:	Durn near killed him
Secretion:	Hiding someplace
Seizure:	Roman emperor
Tablet:	Small table
Terminal illness:	Got sick at the bus station
Tumor:	Adding a couple more
Urine:	Opposite of you're out
Varicose:	Right next to you
Vein:	Metal chicken on your barn room

★★★

Why do liberal Congressmen like it
when a woman blows in their ear?
They're always afraid they're losing
their air pressure.

"Just a little more, Honey.
I did a lot of debating today."

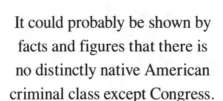

It could probably be shown by
facts and figures that there is
no distinctly native American
criminal class except Congress.

MARK TWAIN

I know a son of a Democrat that got so
excited when he was promoted to third grade
that he cut himself shaving.

At a dinner party, one of the guests was a
Democratic leader being rather noisy
and insufferable. Intending humor, he held
up a piece of meat on the end of his
fork and loudly asked, "Anybody know if
this here is pig?"

Asked a quiet voice from the far end of the
table, "Sir, to which end of the fork do
you refer?"

★★★

I have reached the conclusion that one useless
man is called a disgrace; that two are
called a law firm, and that three or more
become a Congress.

JOHN ADAMS

★★★

Lord, the money we do spend on
Government and it's not one bit better than
the government we got for one-third
the money twenty years ago.

WILL ROGERS

★★★

Two senior citizens were playing bridge
and discussing the recent scandals of
the Democrats. "Can you believe their gall?"
complained the first. "I can't stand this
current kind of conceited and obnoxious
liberal politicians compared to the
old kind."

"What old kind?" asked her friend.

★★★

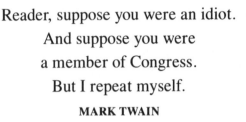

Reader, suppose you were an idiot.
And suppose you were
a member of Congress.
But I repeat myself.

MARK TWAIN

★★★

After a rally, a rural father brought
his offspring up to meet their Democratic
Congressman. "Thirteen children!"
exclaimed the politician. "All good
Democrats, I hope."

"All but one," said the proud father.
"My oldest, Willie, he took to readin' them
newspapers, and we just couldn't keep
him in the fold."

★★★

Any well-established village in New
England or the northern MiddleWest could
afford a town drunkard, a town
atheist, and a few Democrats.

D.W. BROGAN

★★★

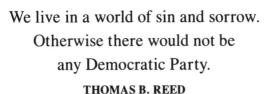

We live in a world of sin and sorrow.
Otherwise there would not be
any Democratic Party.

THOMAS B. REED

★★★

A couple of young Democrats saw a
Republican boy leading a donkey. Thinking
they could have some fun with him, one
yelled out, "Say, boy! You sure are keeping
a tight rein on that brother of yours!"

"Sure am," said the quick-witted boy.
"I'm afraid he's gonna go back and
try to join that liberal Congress again."

★★★

Did you hear about the new lottery the
Democrats are proposing?
Everyone is required to play *every*
week, *nobody* wins, and then they give
themselves a pay raise with the revenue.

★★★

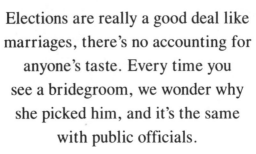

Elections are really a good deal like
marriages, there's no accounting for
anyone's taste. Every time you
see a bridegroom, we wonder why
she picked him, and it's the same
with public officials.

WILL ROGERS

Someone left the cages open at the zoo's
reptile house and snakes went
slithering everywhere. Frantically, the
zookeeper tried everything, but he couldn't
round them up. The zoo director came
down and said, "Quick! Call our
Congressman! He speaks the language!"

If you can't convince them,
confuse them.

HARRY S. TRUMAN

★★★

What's the difference between debating
with a monkey and debating with a liberal?
You get more rational arguments
from the monkey.

★★★

We see our own budgets going up for staff.
There's more staff here than we need.
They're all nice people. But the more staff
you have, the more ideas you have,
and most of them cost money.
I haven't had many staff people
come in with ideas to save money.
It's always some new program to get
their boss out front.

SENATOR ROBERT (BOB) DOLE

★★★

What is the fastest way to change the mind
of a Democrat Congressman? Blow in
his ear until it's all been replaced.

★★★

The receptionist in the office of a leading Democrat Senator picked up the phone. "I need to speak to the head hog," said the caller.

"Sir," she replied, "I hope you don't mean the Senator. In this office we give more respect to the great Democratic leaders of our country. We call him 'Senator,' or 'Mr. Mitchell.'"

"Sorry, lady," he said, "I just wanted to donate $1,000,000 to his reelection fund."

"Just a second," she interrupted, "here comes the pig now."

★★★

There is something about a Republican that you can only stand him for just so long. And on the other hand, there is something about a Democrat that you can't stand him for quite that long.

WILL ROGERS

★★★

It's getting harder and harder to support
the government in the style to which
it has become accustomed.

FARMER'S ALMANAC

★★★

A conservative Senator was opening the
second day of debate on gays in the
military. "Yesterday, we heard a freshman
Senator from the other side of the aisle
talk at length regarding this proposal. She
talked and talked, and then she talked
some more. She talked her head off.
If anyone happens to see it,
please return it to her immediately. I
am told that without it she can barely
operate at half-speed."

★★★

Fleas can be taught nearly anything
that a Congressman can.

MARK TWAIN

★★★

How many people does it take to clean up a waste dump?

Exactly 100. One tractor driver to handle the hazardous waste and 99 environ-mental lawyers to handle the toxic lawsuits.

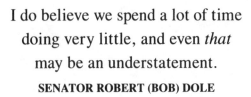

I do believe we spend a lot of time
doing very little, and even *that*
may be an understatement.

SENATOR ROBERT (BOB) DOLE

★★★

I hope the standard of living doesn't go
any higher. I can barely afford
living where it is now.

★★★

The Democrats are in a real bind.
They won't get elected unless things
get worse and things won't get worse
unless they get elected.

JEANNE KIRKPATRICK

★★★

What do Al Gore and a clarinet have
in common? Both are
wooden, wind instruments.

★★★

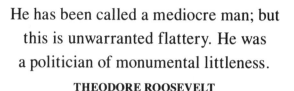

He has been called a mediocre man; but
this is unwarranted flattery. He was
a politician of monumental littleness.

THEODORE ROOSEVELT

★★★

A Republican Congressman was walking
to the podium about to make a speech.
A liberal in the back shouted out, "Tell 'em
all you know. That couldn't take long!"

"How about I tell 'em all we *both*
know?" shot back the Republican. "It
won't take any longer."

★★★

Christmas is a time when kids tell Santa
what they want and adults pay for it.
Deficits are when adults tell the
government what they want—
and their kids pay for it.

RICHARD LAMM

★★★

Bill Clinton was becoming quite worried about his public opinion polls. Seeing Bob Dole at a state dinner, he cornered his Republican adversary.

"Bob, do you think I'm not trustworthy?"

Answered Dole, "Personally, Mr. President, no. But then, what's my opinion against millions of others?"

A congressman is a pig. The only way to get his snout from the trough is to rap it sharply with a stick.
HENRY ADAMS

I never meant to imply that liberals were dumb. What I meant to impart is they just shouldn't tax their mental capacity chewing gum while they're tying their shoes.

★★★

The U.S. Senate may not be the most
refined and deliberative body in existence,
but they've got the most unique rules.
Any member can call anybody in the world
anything he can think of and they can't
answer him, sue him, or fight him.
Our constitution protects aliens, drunks,
and U.S. Senators. There ought to be one
day, just one, where there is an
open season on Senators.

WILL ROGERS

★★★

My Democrat Congressman may have never
had an ulcer himself, but so many
people in his district have one he should be
quarantined as a carrier.

★★★

Blessed are the young,
for they shall inherit
the national debt.

HERBERT HOOVER

★★★

Taxes. Each year that's how the liberal
Congress says, "Stick 'em up!"

★★★

A man was out driving when he noticed
scores of people walking single file
down the median. Hundreds of people
stretched for blocks and blocks. When he
finally reached the front of the proces-
sion, he saw that the people were following
two hearses, behind which were several
limousines. When he noticed Ronald
Reagan in one of the limousines, that was
it—he *had* to know what was going on.
He pulled his car behind the limos, and
followed them to the cemetery. When they
got there, he got out and went over
to Reagan's limousine. Reagan was
stepping out, and had an enormous bear
on a leash.

"Pardon me, Mr. Reagan," said the man,
"but I have never seen a funeral or pro-
cession like this. What's going on?"

"Well," said Reagan, "two of the most liberal Democrats in Congress died. This bear ate them both. Evidently he has a real appetite for liberals."

"Wow," said the man, "I could use a bear like that. Could I borrow him some time?"

"I suppose so," said Reagan, pointing to the file of people strung out to the horizon, "but you'll have to wait in line just like everybody else."

★★★

Peter Marshall, longtime chaplain of the U.S. Senate, was asked by some tourists what exactly were his Congressional responsibilities. "I open each day's Senate business praying for God to grant wisdom for our Senators. Then I take a seat. After listening to some of the ideas of these liberal Senators, I spend the rest of the day praying for America."

★★★

A Democrat Senator was full of himself after giving a speech. "Did you notice how my speech seemed to fill the whole room tonight?"

Replied his Republican colleague, "Well, I did notice that when you started, quite a few people left to make room for it."

★★★

An extremely boring Democrat was giving another typically sleep-worthy speech when someone in the front row started to snore, increasingly loudly. Growing furious, the Democrat grabbed the gavel off the podium, flung it at the culprit, and hit him squarely on the head. Then he continued his speech as if nothing had happened. The startled offender looked up at the Democrat on the platform, closed his eyes, and said, "Quick, hit me again. He's still talking."

★★★

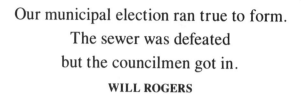

Our municipal election ran true to form.
The sewer was defeated
but the councilmen got in.

WILL ROGERS

★★★

A funeral home called Ronald Reagan to
let him know that an extremely liberal
Supreme Court justice had died.
"How should we dispose of his remains,
Mr. President?" asked the mortician.
"Should he be embalmed, buried, or
cremated?"

"All three," answered Reagan. "Take no
chances."

★★★

The liberals can understand everything but
people who don't understand them.

LENNY BRUCE

★★★

In biblical times it took a divine act for a donkey to speak. Unfortunately, many liberal Congressmen exercise this miracle power every day.

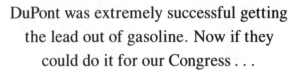

DuPont was extremely successful getting
the lead out of gasoline. Now if they
could do it for our Congress . . .

★★★

People forget ours is a government
of the people, by the people, and
for the people. Too often when these
liberals get into office, they just
do it *to* the people.

★★★

A local Democratic mayoral candidate
was bragging to his opponent how he
was influencing votes. "I give every cab
driver a double-sized tip and then I
tell him, 'Don't forget to vote for me!' "

"I use a slightly different method," said
his wily Republican opponent. "Only
it's cheaper and *a lot* more effective. First,
I totally stiff the cabbie, and then I tell
him to vote for you."

★★★

An election is coming. Universal peace
is declared, and the foxes have a
sincere interest in prolonging the
lives of the poultry.
GEORGE ELIOT

A Democrat Senator was about to speak
to a group of senior citizens. "You
haven't heard nothin' till you've heard
today's speaker," said the host introducing
the orator.

"*Then* you will have heard nothing,"
retorted a heckler.

After giving a campaign speech detailing
his entire platform, a Democratic hopeful
confidently asked, "Are there any questions?"

"Yes," came the voice from the rear. "Is
there *anyone else* running?"

★★★

I know a politician who believes that
there are two sides to every question—
and takes both of them.

KEN MURRAY

★★★

Can there exist a cheaper way to have
your family tree traced than to
run for public office?

★★★

A liberal Congressman walked backstage
after finishing a speech, and the crowd
was going nuts with applause and shouting.
His assistant approached him. "I'm
sorry, sir, I was late getting here, so I didn't
hear whatever you said to receive such a
tremendous ovation. It must have been a
wonderful speech. What did you say?"

Said the fuming politician, "I said I
wouldn't begin my speech until they
quieted down."

★★★

A Democrat Congressman was asked to substitute as a speaker for a colleague. The Democrat began by explaining the meaning of a substitute.

"If you break a window, and replace it with cardboard instead of a pane, that would be a substitute."

After his prattling and perplexing speech was finished, a confused and frustrated woman approached.

"Sir, you need not say you were a substitute. Never in my entire life, have I seen a bigger pane than you."

★★★

Politicians can forgive about anything in the way of abuse. They can forgive subversion, revolution, being contradicted, exposed as liars, even ridiculed, but they can never forgive being ignored.

AUBERON WAUGH

★★★

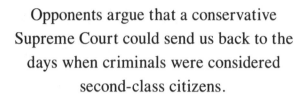

Opponents argue that a conservative Supreme Court could send us back to the days when criminals were considered second-class citizens.

★★★

Economists think the poor need them to tell them that they are poor.

PETER DRUCKER

★★★

One liberal to another: "What does 'coincidence' mean?"

"Funny," said the other, "I was going to ask you the same thing!"

★★★

Bill Clinton is still searching for the perfect White House staff . . . hardworking, loyal, prone to amnesia.

★★★

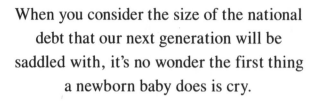

When you consider the size of the national debt that our next generation will be saddled with, it's no wonder the first thing a newborn baby does is cry.

★★★

Man is the only animal that laughs. He's also the only animal that has a legislature.

BETTY ANN DITTEMORE

★★★

The Congress dealing with health care is like a great pack of cockroaches in your kitchen. It's not what they can eat or cart away . . . it's what they fall into and totally pollute.

★★★

No party is as bad as its leaders.

WILL ROGERS

★★★

Bill Clinton is a politician with his feet firmly planted in midair. Whichever way the political winds are blowing is where he lands.

"I don't know how I do it, Michael...
but it sure comes in handy!"

Under current law, it is a crime for a
private citizen to lie to a
government official, but not for the
government official to lie to the people.
DONALD FRASER

★★★

It's hard for our liberal Congress to figure
out how to spend money. For so many
years they've just thrown it away.

★★★

Ask five economists and you'll get
five different explanations.
Six, if one went to Harvard.
EDGAR A. FIEDLER

★★★

Did you hear about the honest Democrat
Congressman? Me, neither.
Probably a rumor.

★★★

Said an egotistical liberal, "I make my living by my wits."

Replied his friend, "I suppose half a living is better than none."

★★★

Politicians are the same all over.
They promise to build a bridge
even when there is no river.
NIKITA KHRUSHCHEV

★★★

Patrick Henry protested taxation without representation. Had he seen our liberal Congress, he'd have realized that taxation *with representation* ain't no great shakes either.

★★★

A liberal is a man too broad minded to take his own side in a quarrel.
ROBERT FROST

★★★

An elected official is one who gets
51 percent of the vote cast by
40 percent of the 60 percent of the
voters who are registered.

DAN BENNETT

★★★

A college girl had just returned home
from a date with the head of a group
of young Democrats.

"How'd it go?" asked her roommate.

"There's was never a dull moment with
that guy . . . it lasted the whole time."

★★★

. . . while the Republicans are smart enough
to make money, the Democrats are
smart enough to get in office every two
or three times a century and
take it away from 'em.

WILL ROGERS

★★★

Their nature, by training and instinct, is to
argue and procrastinate. Yet we persist
in electing lawyers to Congress.

BENJAMIN FRANKLIN

★★★

There was a time when a fool and his
money were soon parted. With the "Tax &
Spend" Democrats running Congress,
now it happens to everybody.

★★★

Did you see Clinton's inaugural party? Only
a blowhard like him would have enough
hot air for that many balloons.

★★★

A billion here, a billion there,
and pretty soon you're talking
about real money.

EVERETT DIRKSEN

★★★

The politicians who make a lastin'
success in politics are the men who are
always loyal to their friends, even up to the
gate of the state prison, if necessary.

GEORGE WASHINGTON PLUNKITT

★★★

When a Democrat says he wants a fair tax
cut, that usually just means he wants
his fair cut of our taxes.

★★★

Congress is where a man gets up to speak,
says nothing, and nobody listens.
Then everyone rises in
disagreement with him.

★★★

In the last few years, the liberal Congress
has made scores of millionaires . . .
of course, they had all been *billionaires*
under Ronald Reagan.

★★★

Diplomats are just as essential to starting
a war as soldiers are for finishing it.
You take diplomacy out of war, and the
thing would fall flat in a week.

WILL ROGERS

★★★

Filling out your tax return every year
should be considered cruel and unusual
punishment. It's sort of like being
kidnapped, forced to write your own
ransom note, paying it to free yourself,
and all the while knowing another
kidnapping is awaiting you next year.

★★★

We're all fuzzy on the issues. That's proven
by the fact that we did get elected. The
advantage of being a presidential candidate
is that you have a much broader range
of issues on which to be fuzzy.

JAMES EARL (JIMMY) CARTER

★★★

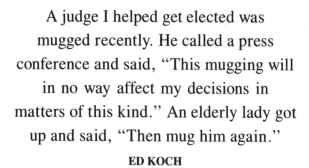

A judge I helped get elected was mugged recently. He called a press conference and said, "This mugging will in no way affect my decisions in matters of this kind." An elderly lady got up and said, "Then mug him again."

ED KOCH

★★★

The Supreme Court has been so liberal for so long, that to fully enjoy your civil rights you'll have to commit a violent crime against society.

★★★

Personally I don't think you can make a lawyer honest by an act of legislature. You've got to work on his conscience. And his lack of conscience is what makes him a lawyer.

WILL ROGERS

★★★

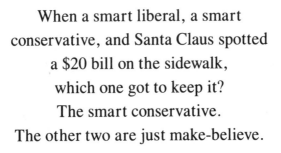

When a smart liberal, a smart
conservative, and Santa Claus spotted
a $20 bill on the sidewalk,
which one got to keep it?
The smart conservative.
The other two are just make-believe.

★★★

The reason you will often see
liberal politicians lost in deep thought
is that they are so rarely in that
neighborhood that they usually can't find
their way back home.

★★★

During a filibuster, one senator threatened
to read the Bible into the [Senate]
Record, and I guess he would have
done it, if only somebody in the
Capitol had owned a Bible.

WILL ROGERS

★★★

Who can understand the anatomy of our
Democrat Congress? They have an
acute abundance of bone in their heads, and
virtually none in their backs.

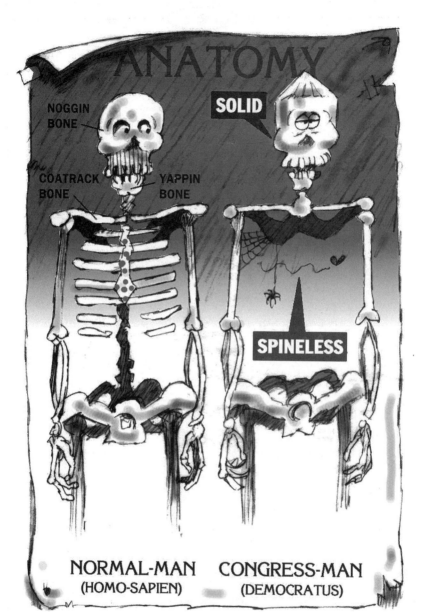

Compassion is the
albatross of the Liberals.

J.B. PRIESTLEY

★★★

Democratic politicians can be hard to work
for. They want everything done
right . . . unless, of course, they're
the one who's doing it.

★★★

Everybody knows that when you die you
can't take your money with you. I just wish
our liberal Congress wouldn't spend so
much time trying to lighten my luggage.

★★★

A politician can do anything as long as he
manipulates the right symbols.

DEMOCRAT GOVERNOR OF CALIFORNIA,

JERRY BROWN

★★★

If they were accurately reported, the
retirements of liberal politicians
would appear in the public improvement
section of the newspaper.

★★★

Two characteristics of government are that
it cannot do anything quickly, and that
it never knows when to quit.

GEORGE STIGLER

★★★

We who are liberal and progressive know
that the poor are our equals in every
sense except that of being equal to us.

LIONEL TRILLING

★★★

One Democrat was so ecstatic about
winning the election that the first thing he
did was inadvertently keep one of his
campaign promises. Ooops!

★★★

The politician is an acrobat.
He keeps his balance by saying
the opposite of what he does.

MAURICE BARRES

★★★

Did you hear about the rose that was
named after Al Gore? It's called the "Gorus
Idiotus," which means "Blooming Idiot."

★★★

The best thing about this
group of candidates is that
only one of them can win.

WILL ROGERS

★★★

Politics is such a torment that I
would advise every one I love
not to mix with it.

THOMAS JEFFERSON

★★★

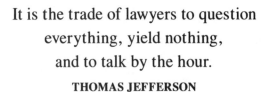

It is the trade of lawyers to question
everything, yield nothing,
and to talk by the hour.

THOMAS JEFFERSON

★★★

Liberals and conservatives basically want
the same thing for the country.
It's just that the liberals want the
conservatives to pay for it.

★★★

I figured why Uncle Sam wears such
a tall hat. It comes in handy
when he passes it around.

SOUPY SALES

★★★

If only we could all invest in tax rates.
They're the only thing that surely
will be going up.

★★★

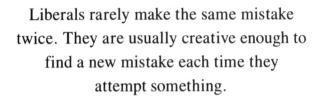

Liberals rarely make the same mistake twice. They are usually creative enough to find a new mistake each time they attempt something.

★★★

Inflation is like sin;
every government denounces it and
every government practices it.

SIR FREDERICK LEITH-ROSS

★★★

I've heard some people say Democratic presidents should serve six-year terms. You just can't expect them to get all their campaign promises broken in four years.

★★★

An honest Democrat is one who,
when bought, stays bought.

HORACE GREELEY

★★★

Politicians give false emphasis to the importance of their work. They read all the political news and suppose everyone else does also.

JOSEPH ELY

★★★

With Congress, every time they make a joke it's a law; and every time they make a law it's a joke.

WILL ROGERS

★★★

If experience teaches us anything at all, it teaches us this: that a good politician, under democracy, is quite as unthinkable as an honest burglar.

H.L. MENCKEN

★★★

The men's room outside the Senate
chambers has a small sign posted over the
hot-air blowers used for drying hands.
"Hand dryers," it reads, "must yield use to
Democrat Senators in need of refills."

"Move over, Bub! The Senator here
needs his daily refill!"

What is the difference between
a carp and a liberal Congressman?
One is a scum-sucking bottom feeder
and the other is just a fish.

★★★

A farmer was anxious to find out how
his 15-year-old son would turn out.

"Mabel," the man announced to his
wife, "I've devised a test that will
determine what he's going to be. Watch
this."

The farmer took out a box and laid its
contents on the kitchen table: a $20 bill, a
Bible, a bottle of whiskey, and a girlie
magazine.

"You see, Mabel, this $20 bill stands for
business, the Bible for the ministry,
and the whiskey and girlie magazine stand
for a life of drunken debauchery. We'll
leave them on the table, go hide, and when
he comes in we'll see how he'll turn out."

The parents hid behind the drapes, and soon enough their son came in and walked over to the display on the table. Examining the items, he picked up the $20 bill, held it to the light, and put it down. Next he picked up the girlie magazine, flipped through it, and put it down. Leafing through the Bible, he uncorked the bottle and took a little sip. The boy then stuffed the twenty in his pocket, tucked the Bible and magazine under his arm, took the bottle, and strolled out of the room.

"Lord above!" exclaimed the farmer. "He's going to be a *DEMOCRAT!*"

★★★

Bedfellows make strange politics.
NEWSCASTER LARRY K. SMITH

★★★

If the Democrat Congress really wants to simplify the tax forms, why don't they just print all the money with their return address on it.
BOB HOPE

★★★

In a movie I saw the other night,
someone reached into a man's chest
and pulled out his still-beating heart.
No doubt the producer probably got
the idea watching Congress voting
the last tax increase.

Politicians' Rules:

(1) When the polls are in your favor, flaunt them;

(2) When the polls are overwhelmingly unfavorable,

    (a) ridicule and dismiss them or

    (b) stress the volatility of public opinion;

(3) When the polls are slightly unfavorable, play for sympathy as a struggling underdog;

(4) When too close to call, be surprised at your own strength.

PAUL DICKSON

★★★

He can compress the most words
into the smallest ideas better
than any man I ever met.

ABRAHAM LINCOLN

★★★

The way things are going, soon the
Congress will "simplify" our
tax form to read, "Whatever you've got,
send it in. You can owe us the rest.
(With interest, of course.)"

★★★

A liberal Democrat came home early
complaining of the flu. "Have you
taken your temperature?" his wife asked.

"I couldn't find the thermometer. All I
could find was the barometer."

"Lemme guess," quipped his wife,
"you're Windy and All Wet?"

★★★

Two men and a Democratic Congressman applied for a job tending 5,000 pigs at a mountaintop pig ranch. The rancher couldn't decide which one to hire, so he sent all three up to give it a go; the best one would get the job.

After the first day, one of the men came down, complaining he couldn't stand the smell of the hogs. The second day, the other man came down complaining he, too, couldn't stand the smell. On the third day, the pigs came down.

★★★

The mother of a liberal Congressman was visiting him in prison after his conviction for accepting a bribe.

"Why didn't you listen to your conscience like I taught you?" she sobbed.

"But, Ma! You also taught me not to talk to a stranger."

★★★

All politicians should have three hats—
one to throw into the ring, one to
talk through, and one to pull
rabbits out of if elected.

CARL SANDBURG

★★★

A little vagueness goes
a long way in this business.

**DEMOCRAT CALIFORNIA GOVERNOR,
EDMUND G. "PAT" BROWN**

★★★

The Democrats raise taxes because they
think people don't have enough
sense to wisely spend their own money.
They think people waste it on food, shelter,
and clothing, when they could be
spending it on new welfare projects, paying
farmers to do nothing, and giving their
Congressmen another raise.

★★★

Franklin Delano Roosevelt
to Bill Clinton:

From a chicken in every pot
to a pot-smoking chicken.

Today, it takes more brains and effort to
make out the income tax form than
it does to make the income.

ALFRED E. NEUMAN

★★★

Bill Clinton was out swimming at the
beach when he was caught in an undertow
and began to drown. Three teenage
boys saw him, swam out, and pulled him
ashore. After regaining his breath,
Clinton said, "Thanks, boys! In
appreciation, I'll use my influence to
help you all in any way I can."

"Great," said the first boy. "I want to go
to West Point!"

"Done," said the president.

"I'd like to go to Annapolis!" said the
second.

"I'll see to it immediately," said the
president.

Downheartedly, the third said, "I want to be buried at Arlington Cemetery."

"What a strange request," said Clinton. "Why on earth do you want to be buried at Arlington Cemetery?"

"Well," said the youngster, "when I get home and tell my father I saved *Bill Clinton* from drowning, he's gonna *kill* me!"

★★★

A conservative Senator was speaking to a bunch of farmers from his state. A Democrat farmer stood up and challenged him.

"Why should I vote for you? You don't know farmers, and you don't know farming. I bet you don't even know how many toes a pig has."

"You're right," said the senator, "but why don't you take off your shoes and we'll give them a count?"

★★★

A cannibal went to his butcher store to get something for dinner. A sign on the wall read: "Professor Brains, $3/lb. Democrat Brains, $100/lb."

"Say," asked the cannibal, "why are Democrat brains so expensive?"

"Supply and demand," said the butcher. "Kill a professor and you'll get 8, maybe 12 pounds of brains. But do you have any idea how many Democrats we have to kill to get just one pound of brains?"

★★★

At a political debate, a liberal Congressman was being forced to defend his voting record. "I am more than happy to stand on my record," he blustered.

"If I had your record," said his opponent, "I wouldn't just stand on it. I would burn the entire thing so NOBODY could read it!"

★★★

I used to say that politics was the
second oldest profession, and I have
come to know that it bears a
gross similarity to the first.

RONALD REAGAN

★★★

Talk about the lunatics running the asylum.
The Congress just voted themselves
another pay raise, saying that it would
motivate them to be more productive.

★★★

What do you want to be a sailor for?
There are greater storms in politics
than you'll ever find at sea. Piracy,
broadsides, blood on the decks—
you'll find them all in politics.

DAVID LLOYD GEORGE

★★★

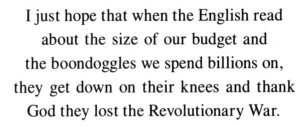

I just hope that when the English read about the size of our budget and the boondoggles we spend billions on, they get down on their knees and thank God they lost the Revolutionary War.

★★★

The Democrats will agree to stop passing the buck as long as they get to keep it.

★★★

A Republican walked into a bar, ordered a beer, and announced loudly, "Hey, I just heard some hilarious Democrat jokes. Anybody want to hear 'em?"

The bartender came over and said sternly, "Listen, Mac. I'm a Democrat. Those two guys to your left are Democrats. See those three truck drivers at the table over there? Democrats. In fact, practically this whole bar is Democrat. You follow what I mean?"

"Sure, I understand," said the Republican. "I'll tell them very slowly, and I promise to not use any big words."

★★★

It is a high honor to be here with you
molders of public opinion. I must
say you've done a wonderful job. I doubt
if public opinion has ever been
as moldy as it is today.

ROBERT STAPP

★★★

Violence has become a great part
of the liberalization of America.
Freeways in California now have places
to pull over and reload.

★★★

A man slipped into a confessional.
"Forgive me, father. Yesterday I killed two
liberal Congressmen."

"I'm not interested in your politics, my
son," answered the priest. "Just tell
me if you've committed any sins."

★★★

A Democrat was trying to get the goat of a young Republican. "I think I'll move to Nevada," he said. "75 percent of Nevadans are Democrats.

"Or maybe Colorado," he went on, "90 percent of Coloradans are Democrats.

"You know, better still," he kept on, "New Mexico. 95 percent of them are good Democrats."

"Well, I'll tell you one thing," said the Republican, "if it's good Democrats you're looking for, you'd better stay clear of heaven."

After a long political career, a local Democratic leader had fallen on hard times and died destitute. Outside the Democrat headquarters, a young volunteer was soliciting donations from passersby. "Excuse me, sir. Would you contribute ten dollars to help bury a lifelong Democrat?"

"Ten bucks?" said the man, "Is that all? Here's a fifty—bury five of them."

★★★

Our politicians are finally learning what *Glasnost* and *Perestroika* mean: "Send money" and "You got any more?"

★★★

Politics does not make strange bedfellows. It only seems that way to those who have not been following the courtship.

KIRKPATRICK SALE

★★★

A ventriloquist was putting on a show for the Democrats in Congress. Naturally, he cracked a few jokes about politicians— singling out the Speaker of the House in particular.

After a couple of these jokes, the Speaker just couldn't take it anymore. "Hey! I'm getting sick and tired of all these jokes about politicians!" he protested. "Not all of us are bad, you know!"

The flustered ventriloquist stammered, "I . . . I'm sorry, sir. It was all in jest. Please don't take it seriously."

"Hey!" snapped the Speaker, "I wasn't talking to you! I was talking to that little smart aleck on your knee!"

★★★

Now I know what a statesman is, he's a dead politician. We need more statesmen.

BOB EDWARDS

★★★

Men play at being God, but lacking God's experience they wind up as politicians.

HARRY WILLIAM KING

★★★

The latest statistics show that 13½ million Americans are not working in any way. Unfortunately, a good many of them have high-paying jobs in the federal government.

★★★

A banker, an electrician, and a Democrat Congressman were all taking an IQ test. One of the questions was, "What word describes the problem of outflow exceeding inflow?"

The banker wrote, "Overdraft."

"Overload," wrote the electrician.

The Democrat wrote, "What problem?"

★★★

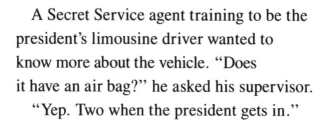

A Secret Service agent training to be the president's limousine driver wanted to know more about the vehicle. "Does it have an air bag?" he asked his supervisor. "Yep. Two when the president gets in."

★★★

Politics, as hopeful men practice it
in the world, consists mainly of
the delusion that a change in form
is a change in substance.

H.L. MENCKEN

★★★

A Republican senator was interviewing a liberal Democrat for a staff position in his office. "I see here," said the senator, "that you were born on April 1. Is that what accounts for your politics?"

★★★

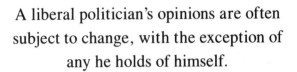

A liberal politician's opinions are often subject to change, with the exception of any he holds of himself.

★★★

Politics is a flexible art. The minute you take a fixed position you're in trouble.

LIBERAL NOVELIST NORMAN MAILER

★★★

Liberal politicians really get a bad rap when you consider that most people have split opinions about them. What I mean is half the time they're despised, and the other half they're only detested.

★★★

Nothing is so admirable in politics as a short memory.

JOHN K. GALBRAITH

★★★

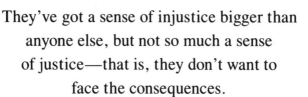

They've got a sense of injustice bigger than
anyone else, but not so much a sense
of justice—that is, they don't want to
face the consequences.

ROMAINE GARY

★★★

NASA has no idea how large space is, and
our Congress no idea how much
money it can absorb.

★★★

Most Democratic politicians say they'll be
tough on criminals . . . except perhaps
those they appoint to their administration.

★★★

The hardest thing in the world to
understand is the income tax.

ALBERT EINSTEIN

A Democrat senator was being shown
through a factory that produced novelty
toys. He stopped at the workbench of a
young man building what looked
like a donkey.

"Say," remarked the Democrat, "why
are you only making the front end of
these donkeys?"

"We only build the front ends, sir," said
the young man. "We ship them off to
Washington for final assembly."

How can you tell a snake from a liberal
politician at a cocktail party? The
snake keeps dropping his drink.

The short memories of American voters is
what keeps our politicians in office.

WILL ROGERS

★★★

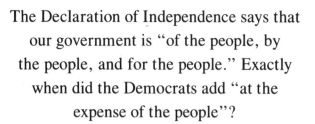

The Declaration of Independence says that our government is "of the people, by the people, and for the people." Exactly when did the Democrats add "at the expense of the people"?

★★★

In politics, as in high finance, duplicity is regarded as a virtue.
MIKHAIL BAKUNIN

★★★

Liberal Congressmen will sometimes tell the truth. Those scoundrels will resort to *anything* to pass their legislation.

★★★

The art of politics consists in knowing precisely when it is necessary to hit an opponent slightly below the belt.
KONRAD ADENAUER

★★★

A liberal Congressman walked into a bar with a pig under his arm. The bartender glanced up at the spectacle and shouted, "HEY! This is a respectable bar! You can't bring that swine in here!"

"But he's *totally* housebroken!" the pig protested.

Republicans have never mastered the
knack, as Democrats seem to have,
of winking while knifing
an opponent's jugular.

JAMES W. NAUGHTON

★★★

How many Democrats does it take to screw
in a light bulb? Just one. He holds the
bulb to the socket and waits for the world
to revolve around him.

★★★

Acting is as old as mankind. Politicians
are actors of the first order.

MARLON BRANDO

★★★

I never give them hell. I just tell
the truth and they think it's hell.

HARRY S. TRUMAN

★★★

I am a man of fixed and unbending
principles, the first of which is
to be flexible at all times.

EVERETT DIRKSEN

★★★

My liberal Congressman recently
participated in a celebrity rodeo, and I had
to see it. Just for once I wanted to see
the bull throwing a Congressman
for a change.

★★★

To err is human; to blame it on
the other party is politics.

★★★

Sooner or later all politicians die of
swallowing their own lies.

CLARE BOOTHE LUCE

★★★

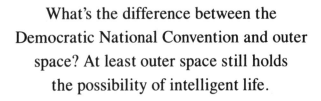

What's the difference between the
Democratic National Convention and outer
space? At least outer space still holds
the possibility of intelligent life.

Each year we give a third of our income to
the Congress so they can send it all
over the globe, to any tiny, depressed
country they deem worthy. That must be
why they call them "*Third* World nations."

Collecting more taxes than is absolutely
necessary is legalized robbery.
CALVIN COOLIDGE

★★★

Why don't snakes bite liberal
Congressmen? Professional courtesy.

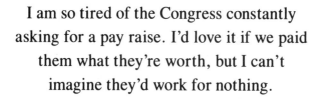

I am so tired of the Congress constantly asking for a pay raise. I'd love it if we paid them what they're worth, but I can't imagine they'd work for nothing.

★★★

Vultures and liberals have a lot in common. Of course, vultures have the courtesy to at least wait until you're *dead* to eat your heart out.

★★★

The Congress is investigating lousy airline service. What a great idea. If anyone knows about lousy service, it's our Congress.

★★★

The point to remember is that what the government gives it must first take away.

JOHN S. COLEMAN

★★★

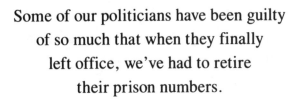

Some of our politicians have been guilty
of so much that when they finally
left office, we've had to retire
their prison numbers.

★★★

A great irony of liberal politics is that when
a politician buys votes with his own
money, he's considered a crook; but when
he buys them with his constituents'
own money, he's a great statesman.

★★★

One day the gate between heaven and
hell broke, and Satan and Saint Peter got
into a big row over who was responsible
for the repairs. Even after much argument
they simply could not reach any agreement.

"Well, then," said Saint Peter, "I'll just
have to get me a lawyer to defend our
heavenly interests."

"And just where are *you* going to find a
lawyer?" queried Satan. "I've got every
one of 'em!"

★★★

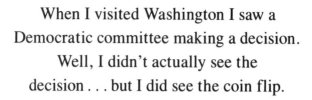

When I visited Washington I saw a Democratic committee making a decision. Well, I didn't actually see the decision . . . but I did see the coin flip.

***

During a campaign stump, an incumbent Democrat senator gave a rousing call to action.

"I want you to vote for me. I want you to vote for honest, ethical, good government!"

Shouted back a wit from the back, "Would you *please* make up your mind?"

***

I looked up "politics" in the dictionary and it's actually a combination of two words: "poli," which means many, and "tics," which means bloodsuckers.

JAY LENO

***

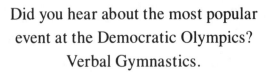

Did you hear about the most popular
event at the Democratic Olympics?
Verbal Gymnastics.

★★★

While these Democrats are not as dumb as
an ox, they're also not much smarter.

★★★

A liberal Democrat was going from
Indian reservation to reservation to get
the Native American vote. At one
reservation he met with a large group of
Indian leaders in the pasture of an
enormous horse ranch.

First he promised new schools and the
Indians shouted, "Ah-loom-pah, ah-
loom-pah!"

When he promised new hospitals and
fully staffed clinics, again the Indians
shouted, "Ah-loom-pah, ah-loom-pah!" and
he was feeling really good about himself.

Finally, he promised new roads, new parks, and financial compensation for all the wrongs of the past. Even louder than before, "AH-LOOM-PAH! AH-LOOM-PAH!" The Democrat was now full of himself, so he finished the speech shouting back, "Yes, ah-loom-pah! AH-LOOM-PAH!"

The tribal chief thanked him. "I appreciate you coming. If you cut through that pasture you can get back to your car, but be careful not to step in any ah-loom-pah."

★★★

After a political argument, a conservative wife offered to wash her liberal husband's hair, and he gladly accepted. The wife started to set up in the kitchen, which bewildered her husband.

"Why are you going to wash my hair in the kitchen sink?" he queried.

"That's where I always wash my vegetables," she answered.

★★★

A local ombudsman was given the chore of
introducing his liberal Congressman.
"You have probably heard of some speakers
that need no introduction. Well, this
guy needs all the introduction he can get."

When she was in college, Hillary Clinton was so confused with her love life she went to a gypsy fortune-teller.

"I want to know who I'm going to marry. I love two boys," she told the gypsy, "Bill and George. Both love me, and both are wonderful. I just don't know who to marry. Can you tell me which one will be the lucky guy?"

The fortune-teller looked deep into her crystal ball, closed her eyes, and pronounced, "You're going to marry Bill. Geroge will be the lucky one."

★★★

The administration keeps renaming things. The MX missile is called a peacemaker. Taxes are now called revenue enhancers. Next thing you know, unemployment will be known as an "unpaid vacation extension."

★★★

Its name is Public Opinion. It is held in reverence. It settles everything. Some think it is the voice of God.

MARK TWAIN

★★★

Ninety-eight percent of the adults in this country are decent, hard-working, honest Americans. It's the other lousy two percent that get all the publicity. But then, we elected them.

LILY TOMLIN

★★★

At the beginning of the year, the Democrats promised the economy would improve when we got to the last quarter. Well, I'm down to my last quarter, and I don't think things have improved that much.

★★★

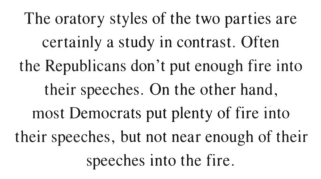

The oratory styles of the two parties are
certainly a study in contrast. Often
the Republicans don't put enough fire into
their speeches. On the other hand,
most Democrats put plenty of fire into
their speeches, but not near enough of their
speeches into the fire.

★★★

These liberal Democrats in Congress
shake your hand *before* the election and
your confidence thereafter.

★★★

You see, ordinarily you have got to work
your way up as a humorist, and first
get into Congress. Then you work your way
up to the Senate and then, if your stuff
is funny enough, it goes into the
Congressional Record.

WILL ROGERS

★★★

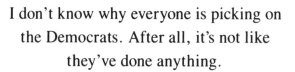

I don't know why everyone is picking on the Democrats. After all, it's not like they've done anything.

★★★

Arthur Hadley's *Do I Make Myself Clear?* gives us the following definitions of "Washington Speak":

"My answer is a definite and final no!"
For the present I'm against it.

"A multimillion-dollar giveaway program."
No money being spent in my district.

"The press has not been entirely accurate in its presentation of this affair."
They've caught me lying.

"I am receiving information from businessmen and labor leaders all over the country that the provisions of this law have proved grossly unfair."
My brother-in-law is in trouble.

★★★

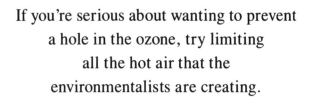

If you're serious about wanting to prevent
a hole in the ozone, try limiting
all the hot air that the
environmentalists are creating.

★★★

A Republican senator was found in
contempt of Congress for calling
the president a cow. When the Senate trial
ended, he apologized to the Senate,
and then asked the Democrat leadership
if, since he now understood he couldn't
call the president a cow, if he could call a
cow a president. The leadership con-
ferred and said that would not be in contempt. He thanked the leadership and
returned to his desk. Before he sat
down, he turned to the president who
had come into the Senate chambers, bowed
elaborately, and sarcastically said, "How
do you do, Mr. President?"

★★★

During a heated debate in the House, a Democrat leader spent the good part of an hour ranting about the Republicans' lack of concern for the homeless. Later during a break, he saw a Republican colleague who chided him for his partisan rhetoric.

"I'm sorry if it seemed partisan," the Democrat apologized, "but the more I spoke, the bigger the head of steam I worked up."

"Yeah, I could see," said the Republican. "The hot air was just pouring out your mouth."

★★★

I sit on a man's back, choking him and making him carry me, and yet assure myself and others that I am very sorry for him and wish to ease his lot by all possible means—except of getting off his back.

LEO TOLSTOY

★★★

With their twisted thinking,
liberals probably think the
best way to combat graffiti
is to sign a *partition*.

"Just sign at the bottom...
and don't forget your address."

One candidate has notified us that his
acceptance speech will be very long.
The other candidate says that his
will be very short. I wonder why one
of them don't announce that his
will be very good?

WILL ROGERS

★★★

A young man moved from a Third World
nation to America. He got a job, and as
soon as he saved some money he sent for
his family to come to America. When
his family arrived, he said to his father, "I
would have sent for you sooner, but
here in America we pay much tax."

His father questioned what taxes were.

"Here, before you get paid for your
work, the government takes part of
your money and you get the rest. The
government is like a great father: It
protects us from enemies, provides an
education for all, cares for the sick, feeds

the hungry, and gives money to those without jobs. The liberal government always wants to do more for us, so it takes our money."

"I understand. It is like having a dog that is hungry. It comes and begs food. I say, 'Dear dog, you are very hungry. I feel sorry for you, so I will give you meat.' Then I cut off the dog's tail, give it to him, and think he will thank me for it."

"Yep," said the son, "you got it."

One morning Bill Clinton brought a golden retriever along with him on his morning jog with his Secret Service agents. As they were jogging, an agent remarked, "That's a beautiful dog, sir."

"Yes it is," replied Clinton. "She's quiet, obedient, faithful—just a great dog. I got it for Hillary."

"Smart trade, sir," offered the agent.

★★★

Bill Clinton has the cleanest mind
in politics. That's because he
changes it every hour.

★★★

Income taxes:
It's Congress's way of
torpedoing your ship
when it finally comes in.

★★★

In *Sidewalks of America*, B.A. Botkin
lists some examples of Washington D.C.'s
special language:

"Confidential Work."
We're so ashamed of what we're
doing that we don't want anyone
to know about it.

"File this."
Lose it, if possible. If anyone calls,
we never heard of [it].

"Have you any remarks?"
Can you give me an idea of what
this is all about?

*"I approach the subject with
an open mind."*
Completely ignorant of the subject.

"In due course."
Never.

"Prepare this for my signature."
You do the work, I'll take the credit,
but if anything goes wrong,
you take the blame.

"Submitted for information."
This means nothing to us.

"This will be borne in mind."
No further action will be taken
till you remind me.

★★★

The secret to Bill Clinton's success boils
down to his ability to show the depth of his
sincerity . . . whether he means it or not.

★★★

Hell hath no fury like a liberal scorned.

DICK GREGORY

★★★

A Democrat was going on a weekend campout with some Democrat friends and invited his Republican roommate to come along. While driving to the campsite, the weather turned, and it became unbearably cold. When they arrived, they noticed that the others had built a roaring fire and were all circled around it. The Republican tried to get near the fire but the Democrats blocked his every effort.

"This fire is for Democrats!" they said.

He said, "You know, last night I dreamed I was in hell." This got their attention.

"Really?" said one of the Democrats. "What was it like?"

"Not much different than right here. I couldn't get anywhere near the fire for all the Democrats in the way."

★★★

A Democrat approached a minister asking for his endorsement in the upcoming election.

"You've asked a difficult thing, and before I decide I'd like to know if you partake in intoxicating beverages."

"Before I answer," said the liberal, "is this an inquiry or an invitation?"

★★★

One thing our Founding Fathers could not foresee—they were farmers, professional men, businessmen giving of their time and effort to an idea that became a country—was a nation governed by professional politicians who had a vested interest in getting reelected. They probably envisioned a fellow serving a couple of hitches and then looking eagerly forward to getting back to the farm.

RONALD REAGAN

★★★

★

Did you hear about the
Clinton-Promise Diet?
You feel no remorse when
you break it.

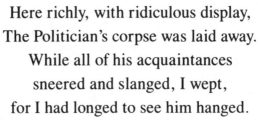

Here richly, with ridiculous display,
The Politician's corpse was laid away.
While all of his acquaintances
sneered and slanged, I wept,
for I had longed to see him hanged.

HILAIRE BELLOC

★★★

There are only three ways to become a
millionaire: inherit money, start a business
and work hard, or get elected to Congress.

★★★

The phrase "to tax a person's thinking"
must be alluring to this pack of liberals
in Congress. Of course, if they could come
up with a way to *actually do it*, they
would be exempt by definition.

★★★

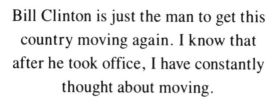

Bill Clinton is just the man to get this country moving again. I know that after he took office, I have constantly thought about moving.

★★★

Things get very lonely in Washington sometimes. The real voice of the great people of America sometimes sounds faint and distant in that strange city. You hear politics until you wish that both parties were smothered in their own gas.

WOODROW WILSON

★★★

You can fool some of the people all of the time. You can fool all of the people some of the time. But you can't fool all of the people all of the time . . . that's what White House press secretaries are for.

★★★

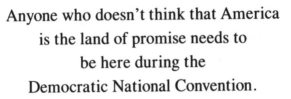

Anyone who doesn't think that America
is the land of promise needs to
be here during the
Democratic National Convention.

★★★

Two conservative senators were discussing the impending debate on health
care, and one was worried that a leading
liberal would not stick to the facts of
the issue.

"I fear that joker is going to murder the
truth."

"Don't worry about it," said his com-
rade. "He never gets close enough to do it
any harm."

★★★

You can lead a man to Congress,
but you can't make him think.
MILTON BERLE

★★★

True to Bill Clinton's campaign promise, his administration has kept a very simple agenda: If it works, regulate it. If you can't regulate it, tax it. If you can't tax it . . . spend a few billion tax dollars on it. Then regulate it.

★★★

A Republican candidate returned home totally exhausted after a long speech-giving tour. Suddenly the Politics Fairy appeared and said he had earned a special wish for all his hard work.

"I will grant any wish," she said, "*but* beware! Whatever you wish for yourself, your opponent will get *twice* as much!"

The conservative sat and thought, and said, "You know, I've been on the road so long I'm half dead. I guess I just wish to stay that way."

★★★

The Rotary Club president was introducing his friend, who was running for governor on the Democrat ticket. "He's the kind of man that can creep into your heart and mind."

A heckler called out, "You're right! I've never met a bigger creep."

★★★

I hear people say the dollar doesn't go very far nowadays. I don't know— a lot of mine travel all the way to Washington each payday.

★★★

New Congressmen spend the first week wondering how they got there and the rest of the time wondering how the other members got there.

SATURDAY EVENING POST

★★★

A doctor, an engineer, and a Democrat were arguing over which of their professions had evolved first. The doctor said, "Medicine is the oldest. Physicians are even mentioned in the Bible."

"That's nothing," said the engineer. "Genesis tells how the world was created from chaos, which obviously couldn't have been accomplished without an engineer."

"Just a second!" said the Democrat. "Who do you think created that chaos?"

★★★

In a free and republican government, you cannot restrain the voice of the multitude. Every man will speak as he thinks or, more properly, without thinking, and consequently will judge effects without attending to their causes.

GEORGE WASHINGTON

★★★

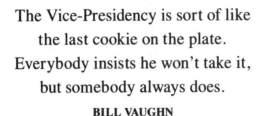

The Vice-Presidency is sort of like
the last cookie on the plate.
Everybody insists he won't take it,
but somebody always does.

BILL VAUGHN

★★★

A filibuster is when a politician talks
endlessly, without ever really
saying anything. Of course, by that
definition, the Democrats *only* filibuster.

★★★

I feel *real secure* knowing that my bank
account is protected by a government that
is six trillion dollars in debt.

★★★

To my mind Judas Iscariot was nothing but
a low, mean, premature Congressman.

MARK TWAIN

★★★

Government is like a baby—an alimentary
canal with a big appetite at one end
and no sense of responsibility at the other.

RONALD REAGAN

★★★

I've heard some Congressmen have taken to
wearing bullet-proof jackets for fear of
assassination. With the kinds of legislation
they've been passing lately, I think
they should try gas masks.

★★★

If God had wanted us to vote, he would
have given us candidates.

JAY LENO

★★★

The president said that inflation has been
arrested. He had better double-check.
I think it just made bail.

★★★

At a cocktail party, a liberal journalist was arrogantly telling a beautiful young Republican woman how he handled himself at such parties.

"Whenever some fool comes up to me and asks me what I do for a living, I sneer and tell him I'm a juggler with the circus. Works every time," he blustered. "So tell me *beautiful*, what do *you* do?"

"Oh, I'm a juggler with the circus," she said as she strolled away.

★★★

All Congressional terms should be ten to twenty with no possibility of parole.

WALT HANDELSMAN

★★★

I can't figure where we're going to put all the crooks and misfits. The prisons and Congress are already full.

★★★

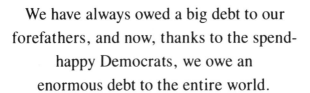

We have always owed a big debt to our
forefathers, and now, thanks to the spend-
happy Democrats, we owe an
enormous debt to the entire world.

★★★

If you want to talk to somebody
who's not busy, call the vice president.
I got plenty of time to talk to
anybody about anything.

WALTER MONDALE

★★★

Generally speaking, the rising population
of the country is a good thing.
The downside is that it also means
more Congressmen.

★★★

One good thing about ignorance: It keeps a
lot of Democrat Congressmen employed.

★★★

Having read some of the recent opinions of
these liberal Supreme Court justices, I
am struck with the belief that if
Lewis Carroll had written another
adventure for Alice, she would have visited
the fantasyland of our High Court
and had conversations with
Justices Tweedle-Dumb and
Tweedle-Dumber-Still.

"ON with his head! ON with his head!"

If a [Congressional] committee is allowed
to discuss a bad idea long enough, it
will inevitably vote to implement the idea
simply because so much work has
already been done on it.

KEN CRUICKSHANK

★★★

Artificial hearts are nothing new.
Politicians have had them for years.

MACK MCGINNIS

★★★

Someone once said that liberal politics was
a promising career. Not until Bill
Clinton did I realize they meant liberal
politics was a career of promising.

★★★

My father was a liberal Congressman.
I, too, have no plans to work.

★★★

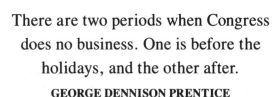

There are two periods when Congress
does no business. One is before the
holidays, and the other after.

GEORGE DENNISON PRENTICE

★★★

The liberal politician's first commandment
is "Thou shall not commit thyself."

★★★

Washington appears to be filled with two
kinds of politicians—those trying to
get an investigation started, and those
trying to get one stopped.

EARL WILSON

★★★

Most liberals are a fun-loving people who
can laugh at themselves. And why
not? Everybody else does.

★★★

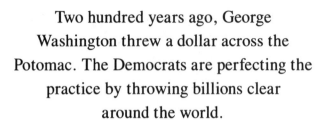

Two hundred years ago, George
Washington threw a dollar across the
Potomac. The Democrats are perfecting the
practice by throwing billions clear
around the world.

★★★

Nobody believes a rumor in Washington
until it's officially denied.

EDWARD CHEYFITZ

★★★

In Clinton's budget, there is something for
everybody. Unfortunately I have a
feeling it's bankruptcy.

★★★

Politics is perhaps the only profession for
which no preparation is thought necessary.

ROBERT LOUIS STEVENSON

★★★

The Democratic party is like a man riding backward in a carriage. It never sees a thing until it has gone by.

BENJAMIN F. BUTLER

★★★

Democratic Congressman are born mountaineers and haven't been on the level since.

★★★

Liberals did not invent crime. They have, however, definitely improved on it.

★★★

Politics is the art of obtaining money from the rich and votes from the poor, on the pretext of protecting each from the other.

OSCAR AMERINGER

★★★

A lifeguard at a country club asked a prospective lifeguard, "Do you know how to save a Democrat from drowning?"

"No, I don't," replied the boy.

"Great, when can you start?"

★★★

Walter Mondale has all the charisma of a speed bump.

WILL DURST

★★★

What's it called when you match wits with a liberal? Solitaire.

★★★

I have made no wild promises [while seeking election], except one— honest government.

ERNEST JOHNSON

★★★

Here lies beneath this mossy stone, a politician who touched a live issue without gloves, and never did come to.

KEITH PRESTON

★★★

With all of the two-faced Democrats in Washington, plastic surgeons there must be making a killing.

★★★

We hang the petty thieves and appoint the great ones to public office.

AESOP

★★★

Being a Democrat politician has tremendous rewards. After you leave office in disgrace, you get to write a book and retire.

★★★

Never poke fun at legislators . . . or
anyone else with the power to route a state
highway through your bedroom.

NOSMO KING

"Sorry, lady, but the governor
rerouted the freeway..."

Once there were two brothers. One ran
away to sea, the other was elected
Vice President, and nothing was heard
of either of them again.

THOMAS MARSHALL

★★★

What do you call a basement full of
liberals? A whine cellar.

★★★

Congressmen and babies should be changed
often . . . and for the same reason.

★★★

Democrat Congressmen are worried about
being replaced by machines.
The way technology is advancing,
how hard could it be to invent
a machine that does nothing?

★★★

What do you get if you cross a rhinoceros, a goose, and a Democrat Congressman?
An animal that at least has the manners to honk before it runs you over and pockets your money.

★★★

A liberal is a person whose interests aren't at stake at the moment.

WILLIS PLAYER

★★★

Politics is the art of looking for trouble, finding it everywhere, diagnosing it wrongly, and applying unsuitable remedies.

SIR ERNEST BENN

★★★

. . . all Congresses and Parliaments have a kindly feeling for idiots and a compassion for them, on account of personal experience and heredity.

MARK TWAIN

★★★

"That was a great job,"
said George Bush to Bill Clinton.
"I appreciate the straightforward way
you dodged each issue."

A phone rings. "Hello?"

"Is this All-American Fertilizer?"

"No, this is the Democrat National Headquarters."

"Well then, I wasn't off by far, was I?"

★★★

I am convinced our ship of state
would be better if there were fewer
liberal pirates on board.

★★★

Politics are very much like taxes. Everybody
is against them, or everybody is for
them, as long as they don't apply to him.

FIORELLO LAGUARDIA

★★★

It's been said talk is cheap; but have you seen
what a session of Congress costs?

★★★

A rumor was being spread around a small community that if the liberals won an upcoming election they might, being against religion, destroy all the Bibles.

An old lady was worried that the Scriptures would become lost for future generations, so she went to the home of a Democrat friend and asked him to hide her Bible. Of course, the Democrat scoffed at the notion, but also wanted to know why she wanted to hide it at *his* house.

"Why, sakes alive, child!" said the lady, "they'd *never* think to go look for a Bible in the house of a liberal!"

★★★

Just because you're a liberal doesn't mean you're odd or abnormal . . . dumb as stone, yes, but not odd or abnormal.

★★★

Politicians get some pretty nice fringe benefits. Of course, when you consider WHO writes the fringes . . .

★★★

A minister and a liberal Congressman both arrived at heaven's pearly gates on the same flight. St. Peter greeted the men and gave each a room assignment.

"Pastor, you've served *long and hard* in service to the Lord. Here are keys to one of our finest efficiency apartments."

Turning to the Congressman, St. Peter continued, "And while you, Congressman, may not have lived a commendable, or even a God-fearing life, we still would like you to have the keys to our finest luxury suite that overlooks the heavenly throne room."

"What's the deal here?" demanded the minister. "I gave my entire life in service to God, while this man spent *his* life in service to *his flesh and sin!* But *HE* gets the luxury suite and view?"

"Listen," said St. Peter pulling the minister aside, "as nice as you are, ministers up here are a dime a dozen. He is the *first* Democrat Congressman we've ever seen."

★★★

A Democrat leader was invited by the Chinese government to come to China and speak on improving American-Sino relations. When he arrived at the auditorium in Beijing, the place was packed. As he started his speech, he noticed a Chinese man behind him at a chalkboard, writing in Chinese.
As the speech progressed, the writing became less and less frequent, until finally the man stopped altogether and took a seat. After finishing his speech, the Democrat asked his host what had been happening.

"Most of the attendees tonight speak very little English," said his host, "so we had this man interpret your speech for them."

"But I don't understand," said the American. "I spoke for over two hours, and he wrote down maybe five things, and nothing in the last 40 minutes."

"Oh," said the host, "that is because we instructed him to only write the good ideas down."

★★★

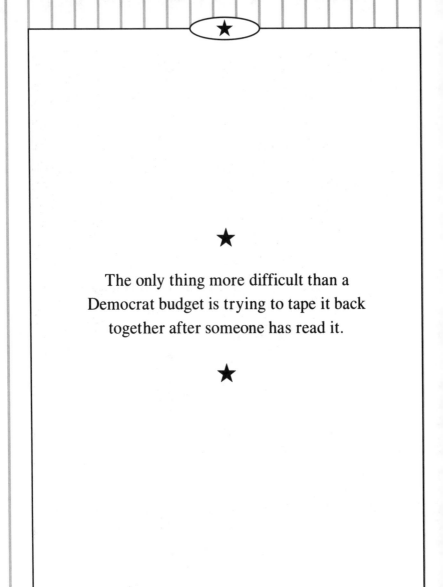

★

The only thing more difficult than a
Democrat budget is trying to tape it back
together after someone has read it.

★

"Look, Bob. If you didn't like it,
you could have just told me."

According to history, the ancient Greeks had an interesting way to discourage silly and stupid legislation. Lawmakers would propose their new laws while standing on a box with a noose around their necks. If the law passed, the rope was removed; if it failed, the box was removed. If we were to try it, though, I don't there could possibly be enough caskets to go around.

★★★

A minister was debating with an agnostic man who didn't believe God punished the wicked.

"In today's paper," said the minister, "is a story about a liberal Congressman who was struck by lightning while he was lying in his bed. Doesn't that sound like miraculous intervention?"

"I don't know," said the agnostic, "it would have been a bigger miracle if it had struck him when he *wasn't* lying!"

★★★

Business is so bad that lobbyists have
been found using food stamps to
bribe their Congressmen.

★★★

As usual, the Liberals offer a mixture
of sound and original ideas. Unfortunately,
none of the sound ideas
are original and none of the original
ideas are sound.

HAROLD MACMILLAN

★★★

Send Us *Your* Jokes!

Do you have some favorite jokes about the liberals in your life? Do you have a better punchline for one of the jokes in this book? Send 'em in—we'd *love* to see them. And who knows? *Your* joke may end up in the next *Liberal Joke Book!* (Of course, we reserve the right to modify any submission as we decide necessary.) Send your jokes to:

—Bob Phillips
c/o Family Services
P.O. Box 9363
Fresno, CA 93702

Other Books by Bob Phillips

- *The All-New Clean Joke Book*
- *Anger Is a Choice*
- *The Awesome Book of Bible Trivia*
- *Awesome Good Clean Jokes for Kids*
- *The Best of the Good Clean Jokes*
- *The Best of the Good Clean Jokes Perpetual Calendar*
- *Bible Brainteasers*
- *Big Book—The Bible—Questions and Answers*
- *Crazy Good Clean Jokes for Kids!*
- *The Delicate Art of Dancing with Porcupines*
- *The Encyclopedia of Good Clean Jokes*
- *Friendship, Love & Laughter*
- *God's Hand Over Hume*
- *Good Clean Jokes for Kids*
- *Goofy Good Clean Jokes for Kids!*
- *The Great Bible Challenge*
- *The Handbook for Headache Relief*
- *How Can I Be Sure? A Pre-Marriage Inventory*
- *Humor Is Tremendous*
- *The Last of the Good Clean Jokes*
- *Loony Good Clean Jokes for Kids!*
- *More Good Clean Jokes*
- *Praise Is a Three-Lettered Word—Joy*
- *Redi-Reference*
- *Redi-Reference Daily Bible Reading Plan*
- *The Return of the Good Clean Jokes*
- *Ultimate Good Clean Jokes for Kids*
- *Wacky Good Clean Jokes for Kids!*
- *Wit and Wisdom*
- *The World's Greatest Collection of Clean Jokes*
- *The World's Greatest Collection of Heavenly Humor*

For information on how to purchase any of the above books, contact your local bookstore or send a self-addressed stamped envelope to:

Family Services
P.O. Box 9363
Fresno, CA 93702